Holiday Doodles

Lucy Bowman

Designed and
illustrated by Non Figg

Edited by Phil Clarke

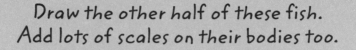

Draw the other half of these fish.
Add lots of scales on their bodies too.

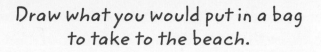

Draw what you would put in a bag
to take to the beach.

Draw a line from the raft to the lake as fast as you can, without touching the sides of the river.

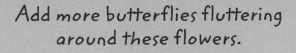

Add more butterflies fluttering
around these flowers.

Draw a line to show which way the campers should go to reach their tent.

Draw windows and doors on the planes.
Add patterns on their tails too.

Fill this chest with treasure, gold and jewels.

Draw a kite on the end of each string.

Doodle things you'd like to eat on a picnic.

Decorate this mermaid's palace with windows, doors and shells.

Draw some of the things you would put in your backpack to take with you on an adventure.

Doodle lots more fish in this aquarium.

Draw the other half of this crab. Try to match the shapes as closely as you can.

Finish your passport photo and add your details,
or those of a character from a book or movie.

•PASSPORT• PASSPORT• PASSPORT• PASSPORT•

FIRST NAME/S

SURNAME

GENDER

NATIONALITY

DATE OF BIRTH

PLACE OF BIRTH

Draw a body, fins and tail on the sea monster.

Give this pirate a hat, an eye patch and
a bushy beard.

Doodle ancient treasures hidden in the pyramid.

Show what the airport scanner reveals inside the suitcase.

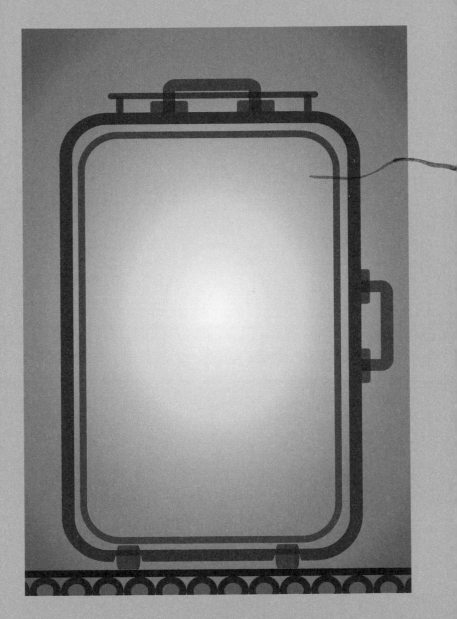

Draw sails on these windsurf boards and yachts.

Doodle patterns on the beach shorts.

Draw around each ring as quickly as you can without touching the prize.

Add stripes to the zebra and
spots to the giraffe.

Draw patterns on
the beach huts.
Add doors and
windows too.

Doodle more footprints on the beach.

Write some postcards to your friends.

Draw something you might spot on a tropical island.

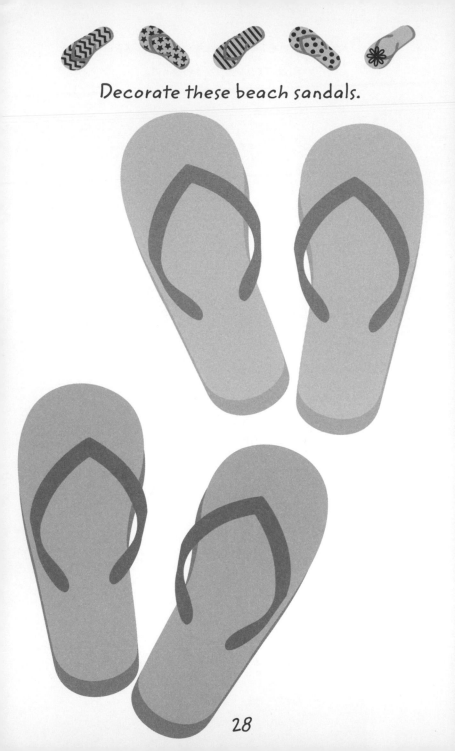

Decorate these beach sandals.

Add lots more penguins.

Draw lots of bags, suitcases and other things on the luggage carousels.

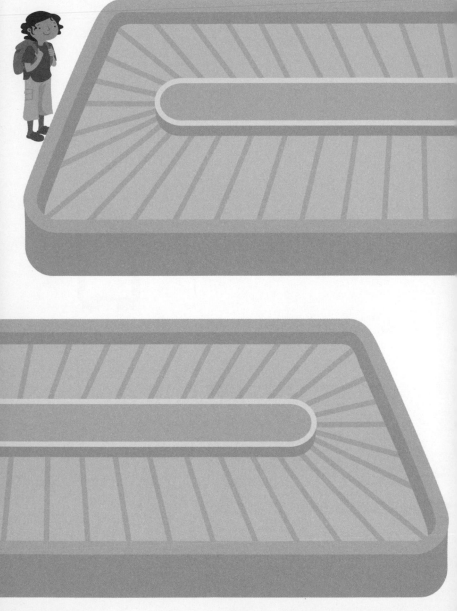

Make each passport photo look different. You could add glasses, long eyelashes or freckles, for instance.

31

Turn these triangles into tents,
kites or sails on boats.

Decorate these sunhats.

Add decorations to the sandcastle.

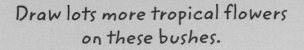

Draw lots more tropical flowers on these bushes.

Doodle patterns on the shells.

What might you see through these binoculars?

Fill the sea with swirling waves.

Draw train tracks winding between the trees.

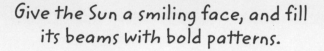

Give the Sun a smiling face, and fill
its beams with bold patterns.

Doodle lots of things in the swimming pool.

Turn these brown shapes into monkeys.

Draw faces on the passengers in this tour bus.

SUNSHINE TOURS

Show what has just swum out of the
cave and surprised the fish.

Decorate this beach towel.

Draw what you think they've caught.

Decorate the ice cream cones with sugar sprinkles and other yummy toppings.

Draw more seagulls in the sky.

Add lots of landmarks to finish this pirate's map.
Remember to add an "X" to mark the treasure.

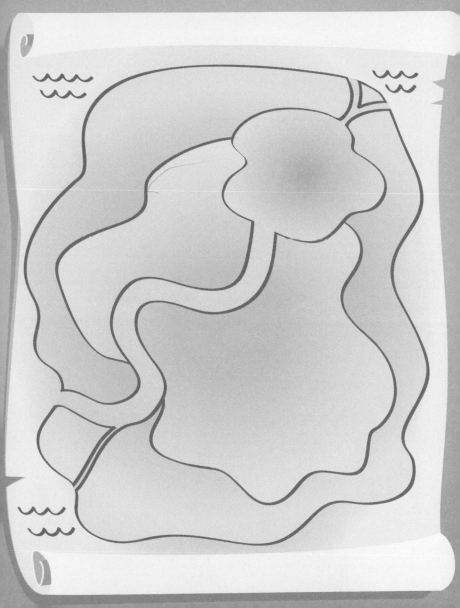

Doodle a face on this tourist, and design a cover for the book.

Draw some passengers in the hot-air balloon.

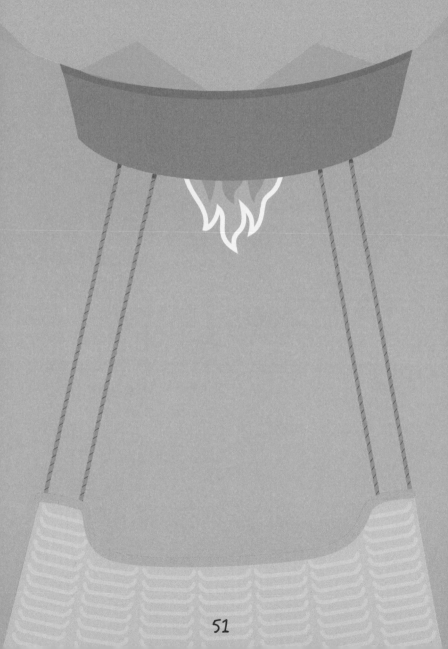

Fill in the shapes with green dots to see some underwater creatures.

Add details to complete these exotic birds.

Draw more dolphins leaping out of the water.

Change the bright shapes into fish.

Doodle designs on the flags.

Today I went to...

and saw a...

Add palm trees to the islands, and sharks in the ocean.

Doodle more tents and people in this campsite.

Personalize your suitcase so you
can't miss it on the carousel.

Build the world's greatest treehouse.

Disguise this man's passport photograph. A beard, a scar or wrinkles, perhaps?

Draw fish, shells and
crabs in the pool.

Decorate the beach balls with spots, stripes, or other patterns.

Draw a scene that you might see through this window.

Who's wearing this sunhat?

Draw a line to lead the diver to the shipwreck.

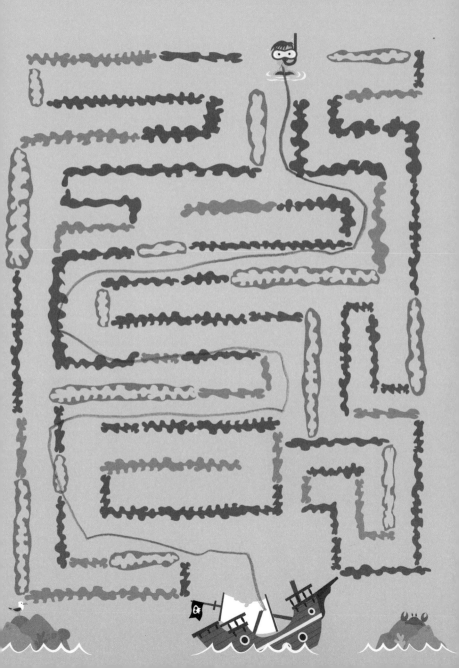

Doodle all the things you'd like to fill
your perfect picnic sandwich.

Decorate the umbrellas,
and draw boots on the people.

Fill these photos with sights
you've seen on your travels.

Draw shells and other things that have
been washed up on this beach.

Turn the shapes below into boats.

Draw the things you would pack for a long sea voyage.

Fill in the shapes with purple dots to see what's hidden in this picture.

Draw a submarine exploring this coral reef.

Finish the face, and add some hair.

Draw what's cooking on this barbecue grill.

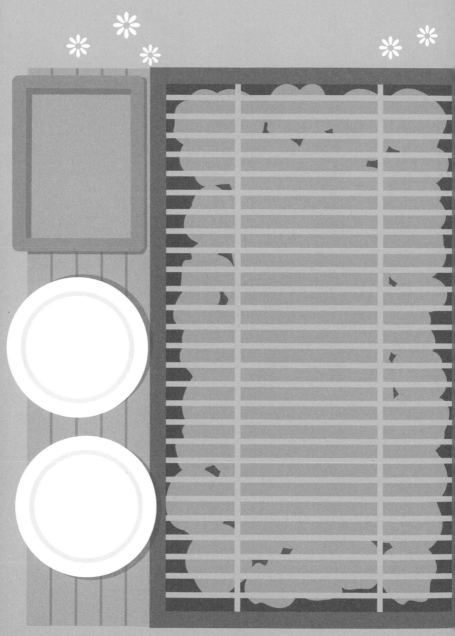

Doodle more crashing, foaming waves.

Give the castle windows, and an impressive gate.

Add more bees buzzing around the flowers.

Decorate these sunglasses for a movie star.

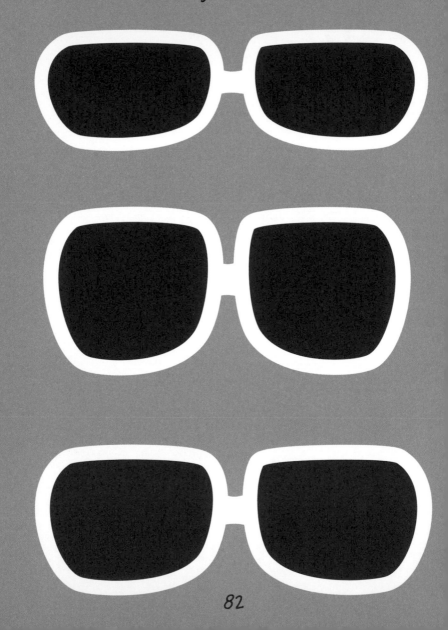

Doodle patterns on the sails.

Finish these fish with eyes, fins and scales.

Add more palm tree silhouettes.

Design some stamps for an exotic country.

Turn these fingerprints into fish, shells and crabs.

Fill in the ticket to your dream destination.

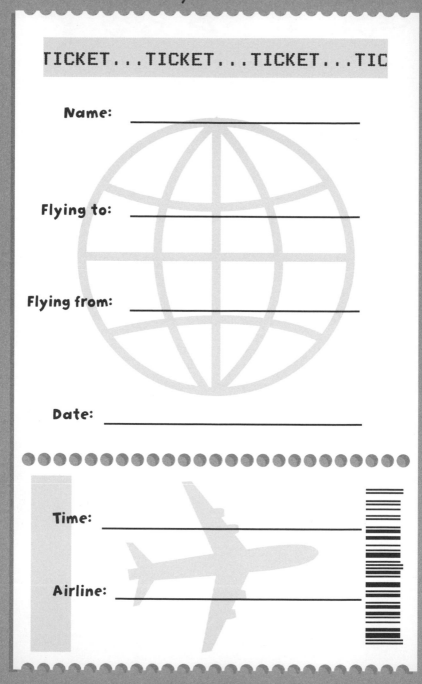

TICKET...TICKET...TICKET...TIC

Name: _____

Flying to: _____

Flying from: _____

Date: _____

Time: _____

Airline: _____

Doodle lots of windows on these skyscrapers and add more buildings too.

Doodle a big sunhat on the dog.

Draw a delicious ice cream sundae in this glass.

Draw two bridges across the ravine.

Doodle faces on everyone at the airport.

Design a souvenir T-shirt from anywhere in the world.

Doodle snorkels and goggles on the divers.

Draw more riders on the roller coaster.

Finish this pirate scene.

Give the mermaid a face and add scales to her tail.

Draw a line that follows the trail with the fewest footprints to the treasure.

Mirror the pattern to finish the surfboard design.

Doodle the rest of this ice cream sundae.

Find the route back to the igloo.

Doodle patterns on the beach towels.

Draw more cable cars with their passengers, and skiers on the mountains.

Doodle patterns on these old temples.

Turn these shapes into a crowd of faces.

Fill in the shapes with red dots to find two creatures you might meet on the beach.

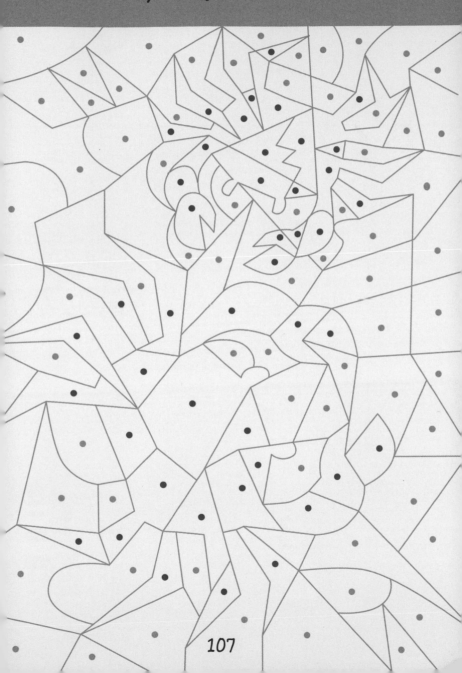

Fill the sky with clouds.

Add windows, doors and passengers to the buses and cars.

Let each souvenir mug celebrate a different destination.

Doodle patterns on the boats and their sails.

Decorate everything before you pack it for your travels.

Additional designs and illustrations by Sharon Cooper

First published in 2016 by Usborne Publishing Ltd, 83–85 Saffron Hill, London ECIN 8RT, England.
Copyright © 2016 Usborne Publishing Ltd. The name Usborne and the devices ♀♀ are Trade Marks of Usborne Publishing Ltd.